Edited by Dorothy A. Hazlin

Designed by Donald G. Paulhus

Text edited by Andrew German

Produced by Fort Church Publishers, Inc.
Little Compton, Rhode Island 02837

Published by and distributed by Mystic Seaport
Museum Stores, Inc., Mystic, Connecticut 06355.

Printed in Japan

NEW ENGLAND HARBORS

Photography and Introduction by
Clyde H. Smith

Text by Waldo C.M. Johnston

INTRODUCTION

When I was a boy growing up in the mountains of New Hampshire, nautical wisdom was not part of my developing lifestyle. Perhaps if I had grown up on the ocean, I would have mastered such things as running an outboard motor, setting lobster traps and navigating foggy shores by the sound of bell buoys. But sailing terminology, such as port and starboard, jib, helm and halyard, were elements of a mariner's vocabulary, not mine. And certainly daily routines regulated by high and low tides were foreign to my sylvan countryside.

I expect the first time I ever learned about a "harbor" was during the Japanese attack on Pearl Harbor in 1941. We did not have TV in those days of course, so communications came mainly by radio, and details a week or two later by newspaper. Pearl Harbor seemed as remote as the moon, but I could tell from my parent's reaction it was serious trouble. Quite suddenly the term "harbor" had special significance even for a youngster living in the mountains.

As the ensuing war escalated, accounts of fierce naval battles somewhere in the South Pacific reverberated over the airwaves. Reports about "tin cans" engaging the enemy on the high seas puzzled me. I wondered about this strange combat with "tin cans," but in time I learned it was a nickname for U.S. Navy warships called destroyers.

Nearly half a century later, while doing photography for this book, I had an opportunity to see one of those "tin cans" up close at a launching ceremony in Bath, Maine. The *Arleigh Burke*, a high-tech supersophisticated destroyer poised like some great leviathan among the shipyard's towering construction cranes adorned in bunting and surrounded by an entourage of dignitaries. The pageantry included Maine's governor, the Secretary of Navy, a cast of admirals, a brass band, and hundreds of beaming Bath Iron Workers. Precisely at high tide, the traditional christening honors were performed by Admiral and Mrs. Burke, and five hundred feet of massive steel roared down the ways and splashed into the Kennebec River!

For many long months the warship evolved from the cradle where its keel was first laid. Many skilled workers labored during those long months to create it. Designers, engineers, machinists, welders, riveters, tinsmiths, electricians, pipefitters, riggers, surveyors, painters, leadmen, other trades unique to shipbuilding – all worked as a team. For such a team of craftsmen launching is an especially proud moment, and I could see it reflected in the multitude gathered by the water's edge. A new warrior, the culmination of dedication and perseverance, bobbed on the surface surging with new life.

As a family of trades and tradition, Bath Iron Works represents generations of committed craftsmen. More than 400 ships have slipped down its ways to the Kennebec during its one hundred-year history. At least eighty of these vessels were those famous "tin cans" from the World War II era.

The evolution of noble fighting ships was impressed upon me once again at Boston Harbor's Fourth of July festivities. Traditionally, the USS *Constitution* is moved from its mooring only once a year to celebrate Independence Day. Riding the ship's wake with a small boat escort, I felt dwarfed by the titanic bulwark of wood and iron. Floating so close to a living relic as it cruised out into the harbor was somewhat like experiencing a time warp. Decorated with an array of banners, pennants and a massive American flag aloft in its rigging, "Old Ironsides" exchanged a volley of cannon fire with Fort Independence where thousands of spectators had gathered. Then the ship, like a ghost from the past, emerged from the cloud of blue cannon smoke and returned to its dock. I wondered if the craftsmen who labored to construct this mighty frigate had shared the same surge of pride at its launching as I had seen on the faces of Bath Iron Workers.

Pride and tradition – those are the special qualities I found time and again while exploring thousands of miles of New England shoreline searching myriad harbors. Certainly those esteemed values sliced the waves of Narragansett Bay out of Newport, Rhode Island, when I followed the super sailing yachts *Shamrock V* and *Endeavour.* With masts towering as high as a sixteen-story building, the legendary J Boats are surely grace on the wind! Once the queens of America's Cup competition, the J's have not raced in America since 1937. The regatta I witnessed, however, was more of a friendly duel between nobility, and when their enormous spinnakers blossomed before the wind, the experience was nothing less than breathtaking! Participating in the return of these classic boats to Rhode Island Sound was one of the most exhilarating events of my photographic adventure.

Harbors are the heartbeat of coastal communities. Here among the assortment of boats, wharves and activities I hoped to capture the intrinsic spirit of those whose lives conform to the sea's perpetual ebb and flow. Perhaps one of the most colorful events is the Blessing of the Fleet in Stonington, Connecticut. Glittering with adornment, the Portuguese fishing fleet is lavishly decorated from bow to stern. Festivities include a rousing parade of homemade floats, marching bands and local fanfare through narrow village streets. Then everyone assembles at the waterfront where the fishing fleet passes before the bishop who blesses each vessel with holy water. Finally the procession proceeds to the mouth of the harbor, where a wreath is deposited upon the water's surface for all to circumnavigate – for good fortune – before returning to port.

For a polychromatic event with a different flare, I attended the annual parade of balloons across Long Island Sound. Launched simultaneously at sunrise near the harbor at Norwalk, Connecticut, the bulging balloons drift out over the water like a string of lollipops. Flying above them, I marveled at the patterns etched on the water's surface by zigzagging chase boats punctuated by the many multi-colored spheres. There is something about a balloon that transcends everyday life. Perhaps it's the gentle rise from our earthly bounds, seemingly without effort. Perhaps it's an illusion of mind over gravitation – a new perspective of our surroundings. Or maybe, it's like eating ice cream – it makes us smile.

Shooting from aloft is my preferred modus operandi. Aside from enjoying the flying experience, I find the aerial perspective best for grasping the landscape's overall character. At Rockland, Maine, I worked with the folks at Owls Head Transportation Museum in a classic 1931 Waco F biplane. Filming from an open cockpit aircraft offers a whole new panorama in which you perceive a closer relationship to your surroundings. Flying in tandem between a 1917 Curtiss "Jenny," a World War I Fokker triplane and a 1912 Curtiss Pusher, we sailed by Owls Head Lighthouse at low level. Ahead, two Russian trawlers lay at anchor just outside Rockland Harbor where local fishermen were selling their catch. In unison we swooped by the Russians in our antique aircraft so close I could see puzzled expressions on the deckhands. Some looked like they were about to scramble for cover under the hammer and sickle. Now, I thought, if only that ancient frigate, "Old Ironsides," should materialize and fire off a few rounds of gunpowder, we'd surely have us an international incident!

New England pride comes in small packages too. I found it in countless boatyards all along the coast. Some craftsmen specialize in lobster boats, those indomitable vessels, so characteristic of New England, which can withstand some of the severest storms. I decided to visit an old friend, David Stainton, on Great Cranberry Island in Maine. A retired architect, Dave now pursues his lifelong dream of designing and building small boats. The results of his craftsmanship are moored in many harbors along Maine's rugged coast. A fisherman's livelihood depends upon the reliability of his boat – the durable lobster boat is certainly one of the finest examples of pride and tradition and can be found in nearly every harbor throughout New England.

When we think of seaports, we often forget there are fresh-water harbors too. New Hampshire's sprawling Lake Winnipesaukee is ringed with seasonal marinas scattered among its sheltered coves and lakeshore villages. And, New England's only interior state, Vermont, shares Lake Champlain with its western neighbor, New York State. Sometimes referred to as "the other Great Lake," the 120-mile-long sliver is squeezed between the Adirondack Mountains on its western flank and the Green Mountains to the east. Most of its harbors and marinas are seasonal as well since the lake usually freezes solid in winter. The only exception is the winter ferry system at Grand Isle where ferry boats loaded with vehicles and passengers navigate a ribbon of open water much like an Arctic icebreaker. Crossing Champlain's broken ice cakes is an experience unique in all of New England.

Whether it's a lobsterman from Machias, a shrimper from Gloucester, a yachtsman from Southport or a ferry boat captain on Lake Champlain, I would have to say they all have one thing in common . . . home is where the harbor is . . . and the harbor is heart. In my travels I came to feel that a stubborn Yankee independent spirit was an essential element of these shoreline communities. Full of pride, steeped in tradition, as solid as "Old Ironsides" herself, as enduring as the granite ledges that frame its harbors, this Yankee spirit is the single ingredient that characterizes New England harbors.

In many ways the release of this book, *New England Harbors*, shares the symbolism of the launching I witnessed in Maine. It, like the ship, represents a culmination of dedication and skills from many individuals. I could not have completed this work without the helpful assistance of many friends – I thank you one and all! I am especially grateful to Tom Aageson, President of Mystic Seaport Museum Stores, for his vision and support. And speaking of pride and tradition, there's probably no finer concentration of these qualities than at Mystic Seaport.

Finally, and most of all, I am indebted to my long time friend and skillful editor, James B. Patrick, who continues to have faith in my work. In striving for the pursuit of excellence, I owe my deepest respect to him for perseverance and perfection. Without his talents and vision, my efforts only amount to a big pile of pictures.

Clyde H. Smith

Well-protected Malletts Bay, just above Burlington on the Vermont shore of Lake Champlain, harbors
yachts large and small amidst the beautiful Vermont countryside.

For 250 years following its discovery by its namesake in 1609, Lake Champlain was
the principal highway between New York and Montreal. Frequently fought over in centuries gone
by, this hundred-mile band of water, with New York's Adirondack Mountains forming a
spectacular backdrop, now attracts those seeking waterborne recreation, and perhaps a bit of history,
as at the Shelburne Museum.

Where the Piscataqua River floods to the sea, Portsmouth has served as New Hampshire's only deep-water port since the 1600s. As modern freighters and navy vessels arrive and depart, they tower over Strawberry Banke, the preserved section of Portsmouth's eighteenth-century maritime community.

One of New England's charming freshwater ports, Wolfboro is the largest town on New Hampshire's largest lake, Lake Winnipesaukee.

At the northwestern end of Blue Hill Bay lies the charming, unspoiled village that borders Blue Hill
Harbor. Here an ever-changing panorama of lobsterboats and yachts complements the
natural splendor of cavorting seals, tree-clad islands, and in the distance the peaks of Mount Desert
and Cadillac Mountain.

With its quiet ambiance, Tenants Harbor on the southwestern shore of Penobscot Bay is a favorite port of call for yachtsmen heading down east to the Bay's fabulous cruising grounds.

A century ago, granite quarries were the mainstay of Vinalhaven's economy, providing the magnificent stone used in so many monumental buildings in East Coast cities. With the decline of the granite industry, island residents turned back to the sea, and at Carver's Harbor the fleet of staunch lobster and fishing boats, busy fish processing plants, and tidy homes reflect the community's industry and dedication to fishing.

Personifying Maine's elemental link with the sea, Spruce Head Cove on Sprucehead Island in the Muscle Ridge Channel serves a small fleet of lobster boats. Here a lobster boat approaches a floating dock, which accommodates for the 9-foot tidal range in Penobscot Bay.

Blessed with one of the finest harbors in Maine, Boothbay boasts a long history of shipbuilding and fishing, beginning in colonial days, when the British and French fought over Maine. Through the decades, Boothbay has prospered and kept up with modern development as summer visitors discovered it. Today fishing boats and yachts share its picturesque, island-filled harbor.

To many of us sailors, Camden is the most beautiful village in America. Tucked between Penobscot Bay and Mount Battie, Camden is both a showplace of eighteenth- and nineteenth-century homes and a thriving modern boating and cultural center. Coming in by sea past Curtis Island and its guardian light, one first sees the church steeples etched against the Camden Hills and the harbor crowded with boats sleeping on their moorings.

New Harbor is a tiny indentation on the eastern shore of Pemaquid Neck facing Muscongus Bay.
Still little altered by development, New Harbor remains a quintessential Maine fishing community,
harboring a fleet that fishes for lobsters, mackerel, haddock, and herring.

During the first half of the twentieth century, Bar Harbor, on the east side of spectacular Mount Desert Island, rivaled Newport, Rhode Island, as the summer social center for the wealthy of the Northeast. Though the large and elegant yachts are gone, the neighborhood still boasts of many lavish mansions. Today, Bar Harbor is more popular than ever as a tourist destination. It is also the home of the Roscoe B. Jackson Memorial Laboratory, a world-famous mammalian research center.

Situated on a spit in Passamaquoddy Bay, up against Maine's border with New Brunswick, Eastport is the nation's easternmost deep-water port, and from it freighters carry forest products and fish to ports throughout the world. Contrary to popular belief, however, Eastport is not the easternmost community in the continental United States; Lubec, a few miles to the south, claims that honor by a few yards.

On the western shore of the Schoodic Peninsula lies the quiet fishing village called Winter Harbor. For most of the year Winter Harbor goes about its business of fishing; but every August the town erupts during the Annual Winter Harbor Lobster Festival, which draws thousands of participants and spectators from all over the East Coast to witness the thrilling Indianapolis 500 of lobsterboat races.

Typical of the many small yards in Maine, Cranberry Island boatyard caters to the repair and storage of small fishing craft and private yachts. With a legacy of excellence, these yards are manned by skilled shipwrights whose workmanship is without peer in the New World.

Snug and picturesque York Harbor, at the mouth of the York River, is the best harbor along Maine's
sandy coast west of Portland. This village in the seventeenth-century town of York has been
a summer resort of Bostonians for generations, and their cottages, with spacious verandas facing the
sea, march along the cliffs on either side of the harbor entrance. Several miles up the coast,
Cape Neddick Light, fondly referred to as "The Nubble" by local residents, serves as a useful bearing
for mariners approaching York Harbor.

This picturesque little village, located where the Harraseeket River empties into Casco Bay, has a rich shipbuilding tradition reaching back more than two centuries and carried on today by descendents of those early shipwrights.

With its spacious harbor sheltered behind the islands of Casco Bay, Portland is Maine's premier port city. During 250 years it has survived several major fires and declines to become a charming model of downtown restoration success.

On Deer Isle in Penobscot Bay, facing the Deer Island Thoroughfare, is the fishing port of Stonington. Here the Billings Shipyard repairs large seiners and trawlers while the local lobster and herring boats share the waterfront with passing yachts and frequent visitors like the schooner *Bowdoin*. Built in 1921 as an Arctic exploration vessel for Admiral Donald McMillan, the *Bowdoin* is now used as a training vessel by the Maine Maritime Academy at Castine.

Located ten miles above the mouth of the mighty Kennebec River, Bath personifies the Maine shipbuilding industry. For more than 350 years the region has built ships. The beautiful houses in Bath were built by shipwrights; the city's Maine Maritime Museum displays its renowned collections at the former Percy & Small Shipyard; and in the heart of the city the Bath Iron Works continues its long and proud heritage as one of America's most progressive shipyards.

Rockland, the largest and busiest Maine port east of Portland, has always been a town more productive than charming. Once lime kilns lined its shore; now it is a hard-working fishing port, which is said to ship more lobsters than any other port in the world.

Located in the grip of rugged Cape Ann, Gloucester was already an active fishing settlement when the Pilgrims landed down the coast at Plymouth. For nearly three centuries it has reigned as codfish capital of the world, and its colorful ethnic mix bears witness to the legacy of those who go down to the sea in ships. No museum of past glories, Gloucester still sounds and smells like a seaport, and its harbor buzzes with activity day and night as seiners and trawlers depart and return from the sea.

The quaint fishing settlement at Menemsha Pond, near Gay Head on Martha's Vineyard,
dates from the late 1800s. The tidy cottages of Menemsha are still occupied by fishermen whose
boats crowd the tiny harbor.

Cohasset is a lovely village on the bulge of the "South Shore" below Boston. Though barely beyond the urban sprawl, Cohasset is a lobstering port as well as a yachting haven. Just offshore is a fearsome array of rocks, including the awesome Minots Ledge.

Located on the southwest tip of Cape Cod,
Woods Hole takes its name from the churning
tidal gut that separates the Cape from Naushon
Island. In the course of 150 years, Woods Hole
has changed from a fishing village to a summer
resort to its modern form as a leading marine
research community.

Since the Pilgrims first landed there in 1620, Provincetown, at the tip of Cape Cod, has been peopled by wanderers. Long known as a fishing and whaling port, this colorful community today freely mixes Portuguese and Yankee fishermen, artists, craftspeople, and nature lovers, old and young. Provincetown skippers now go whaling with cameras rather than harpoons, carrying boatloads of visitors out to watch whales on the nearby feeding grounds.

Located among the tidal estuaries of southeastern Massachusetts, behind the sweep of Horseneck Beach, Westport offers the quiet attractions of a summer by the shore.

Tiny Cuttyhunk, at the end of the Elizabeth Islands chain, claims to be the site of Bartholomew Gosnold's 1602 settlement. Today, its little village of Gosnold is shared by year-round natives and many summering families who have come to Cuttyhunk for generations and whose love for this quiet, beautiful place runs deep.

Much of Nantucket's 350 years of history is evident in the twisting streets of this island community, thirty miles south of Cape Cod. As the first queen of American whaling ports, the Quaker town prospered, and the elegant mansions of the captains and shipowners bespeak its success. A century of genteel decline preserved the town's nineteenth-century character, and even its cobbled streets, until a new generation discovered its charms and filled its harbor with yachts.

Halfway between Boston and Plymouth, picturesque Scituate harbor offers the best protection in foul
weather between the Cape Cod Canal and Gloucester. Even when visiting yachts crowd their
fishing and pleasure boats, Scituate residents remain welcoming and friendly.

Since its founding in the eighteenth century, where the Acushnet River empties into Buzzard's Bay, New
Bedford has been a hard-working community. For decades it was the world's leading whaling port,
and its fleet of hundreds of whaleships prowled the seven seas for years at a time. Whaling profits fed
a burgeoning local textile industry, but whaling and textiles are gone now. Smaller, older Fairhaven
across the river retains traces of its nineteenth-century appearance, not far changed from when
Herman Melville departed there on his whaling voyage. In this century New Bedford and Fairhaven
have found new life as fishing ports, and their fleet of scallopers and draggers rivals that of Gloucester.

Facing Chappaquiddick Island on Martha's Vineyard, Edgartown has made the transition from a whaling and fishing port to a yachting center that rivals Newport. The Edgartown Yacht Club is the focal point of this intense yachting activity. The town's handsome homes reflect its 350 years of history. Many are crowned by traditional widow's walks, yet their immaculate gardens lend a pastoral quality to this saltwater community.

Sheltered from the northeast by Cape Ann, Salem has been a port since the 1600s, but even today it is
best known for its infamous witch-hunt and trials in 1692. After the Revolution, Salem captains
ventured to all corners of the globe seeking to trade, and in 1799 masters who had rounded Cape Horn
or the Cape of Good Hope founded an exclusive club, the East India Marine Society. "Curiosities"
they brought back from their Pacific travels today form the core of the maritime collections at the
world-renowned Peabody Museum of Salem. On the waterfront nearby, the National Park Service
preserves the custom house where once Nathaniel Hawthorne worked.

On a rocky cove, where the Atlantic Ocean thunders against Cape Ann, lies the tidy village of Rockport.
Rockport was born as a colonial fishing settlement, flourished as the granite ribs of Cape Ann
were harvested for urban construction, and survives as a popular haven for artists who
come to interpret the waterfront's picturesque motifs.

In a bight at the north end of the island lies Vineyard Haven, the main port of Martha's Vineyard.
The town's charm is nearly overlooked amidst the bustle of visitors coming and going aboard
the big ferries that connect the island with Woods Hole on Cape Cod.

There is no place in the world quite like Marblehead. For 350 years this little port just below
Salem has had intimate links to the sea, and today it is virtually a living museum, its narrow crooked
streets lined with colonial homes and quaint shops. But its focus still remains the harbor,
which is crammed with sailing craft and graced with the clubhouses of three famous yacht clubs,
the Boston, Eastern, and Corinthian.

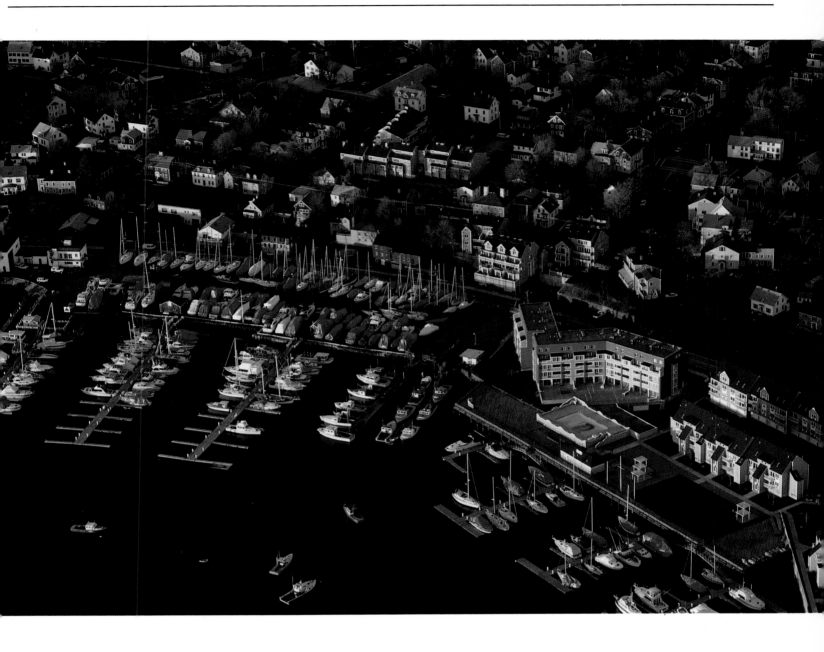

Settled before 1630, across the Danvers River from Salem, Beverly mixes eighteenth- and twentieth-century charm in its ongoing links to the sea.

New England's greatest seaport since the 1630s, Boston has rebuilt and reshaped its waterfront numerous times through the centuries. Shifts in its maritime trades left much of the waterfront neglected during recent decades, but now Boston has rediscovered its links to the sea. In a remarkable transformation, the community has renovated old commercial buildings as residences and shops, bringing new life and spirit to the harborside and filling the old commercial docks with yachts.

Fronting Nantucket Sound on the south coast of Cape Cod, Hyannis strains to contain all of its maritime activity, from fishing boats and Nantucket ferries to sailing dinghies, in a narrow and twisting harbor.

The rockbound shore and ledges of Sakonnet Point, at the mouth of the Sakonnet River in the southeastern corner of Rhode Island, received its warning lighthouse in 1884. Just inside the river's mouth, the unspoiled village of Sakonnet, shared by fishermen and long-time summer residents, has a picturesque little harbor jammed with fishing and lobster boats.

On Aquidneck Island in lower Narragansett Bay, Newport has a rich heritage of seafaring. A leading
American seaport before the American Revolution, Newport became a summer colony of lavish
estates for the fabulously rich after the Civil War, and for the last century has been perhaps the yachting
capital of America. In Newport, one can step easily from the twentieth to the eighteenth century
amidst the narrow streets of tastefully restored colonial homes, and though its spacious harbor is
filled with yachts, one can still find fishing boats berthed along its reborn waterfront.

Block Island is named for America's first "yachtsman," Adriaen Block, who cruised these waters
in what the Dutch called a yaacht and visited the island in 1614. The island remained an isolated
fishing colony until tourists discovered it in the 1870s. When a breakwater created the island's first
all-weather harbor, the community prospered. Today, the large wooden hotels of a century ago
still purvey the simple charms of that era.

Along the meandering estuary of the Warren River in upper Narragansett Bay, the centuries-old communities of Barrington on the west shore and Warren on the east share a passion for sailing. Clubs such as the Barrington Yacht Club and the Edgewood Yacht Club, a few miles up the Bay, promote active sailing programs on Narragansett Bay.

At the southwestern tip of Rhode Island, Watch Hill is the "starting gate" for boats bound east to Block Island, Newport, the Elizabeth Islands, and beyond. Since 1807 its lighthouse has marked the treacherous entrance to Fishers Island Sound. Watch Hill became a summer resort late in the nineteenth century, when city folk discovered the charm of its breezes and its ocean beaches.

Tucked up inside Point Judith Pond, and protected by the harbor of refuge breakwaters at this hazardous midpoint on the Rhode Island coast, lies Galilee. Since the port was constructed early in this century, it has become an important fishing community.

A bit of Colonial America is preserved in the little port of Wickford, on the western shore of
Narragansett Bay. With one of the finest harbors along the Bay, Wickford has been married to the
sea for more than three centuries. Its small trading fleet is long gone, but today Wickford offers all the
charm and every convenience and necessity a yachtsman could want.

Along the narrows of the tidal Mystic River, three miles above its entrance into Fishers Island Sound,
lies the village of Mystic. In the nineteenth century Mystic was a renowned shipbuilding center,
and the homes of its shipwrights and shipmasters, now restored, still grace the community.
Today, Mystic is best known as the home of the internationally famous Mystic Seaport Museum,
founded in 1929. Queen of the Museum's watercraft is the 1841 New Bedford whaleship
Charles W. Morgan, the last survivor of her kind.

Westbrook epitomizes the popularity of boating today. Commanding craft of varying shapes and materials, many more pleasure-seeking seafarers depart the modern harbor of Westbrook than ever did during the three centuries since its founding.

At the mouth of the little Mill River, just west of Fairfield, the tiny harbor of Southport can offer either secure refuge in foul weather or the timeless beauty of a quiet dusk.

After nearly 350 years, New London still looks seaward down the Thames River. Connecticut's leading colonial port, New London was burned by Benedict Arnold in 1781, but arose to become America's second leading whaling port by the 1840s. Today, the U.S. Navy's man-made leviathans – nuclear submarines – are built and berthed along the Thames, and the U.S. Coast Guard Academy calls New London home.

Looking almost like a village transplanted from the Maine coast, Noank sits astride a rocky point at the mouth of the Mystic River. This little fishing community flourished as a shipbuilding center late in the nineteenth century, and many of its homes reflect the art of the shipwright.

The light breezes of western Long Island Sound are often more suitable for balloonists than for sailors, but the Norwalk Islands are a picturesque place to drift. Once oyster boats abounded here; now pleasure craft have taken their places.

Once its harbor sheltered small trading schooners and oyster boats, but Fairfield, just west of
Bridgeport, is now a bedroom community for the expanding commercial metropolis of New York.
Western Long Island Sound has perhaps the densest population of pleasure boats in all of America,
and a share of them call Fairfield home port.

The commercial ramparts of Stamford look out on a harbor that has seen 350 years of maritime activity. The wooden schooner and concrete office tower personify the past and future of many New England ports.

Located on a neck in the southeastern corner of Connecticut, the port of Stonington has quick access to Block Island Sound and the Atlantic. This explains its prosperity as a trading, whaling, and steamboat port in the nineteenth century and as an active fishing port today. Handsome homes bear witness to Stonington's earlier maritime successes, while the annual Blessing of the Fleet embodies the hopes and fears of its Portuguese fishing families.

The lovely old village of Essex remains a sailor's town, though it is located nearly ten miles
up the beautiful Connecticut River. Essex marinas and moorings are occupied by the boats
of serious sailors, and the seagoing atmosphere even pervades the Griswold Inn, which has been
in continuous operation since 1776.